SPECTRUM®
READERS

GO WILD!

African Safari

By Lisa Kurkov

Carson-Dellosa
Publishing

SPECTRUM®

An imprint of Carson-Dellosa Publishing, LLC
P.O. Box 35665
Greensboro, NC 27425-5665

© 2014, Carson-Dellosa Publishing, LLC. Except as permitted under
the United States Copyright Act, no part of this publication may
be reproduced, stored, or distributed in any form or by any means
(mechanically, electronically, recording, etc.) without the prior written
consent of Carson-Dellosa Publishing, LLC. Spectrum is an imprint of
Carson-Dellosa Publishing, LLC.

carsondellosa.com

Printed in the USA. All rights reserved.
ISBN 978-1-4838-0116-2

01-002141120

The truck is packed.
We are ready to go.
We will see animals
in the wild.
We are on an African safari!

Guide

Look over there!
I see our guide.
He is searching for animals.
What will we see first?

Leopard

Look over there!
I see a leopard.
Leopards climb trees well.
Their spots help them hide.

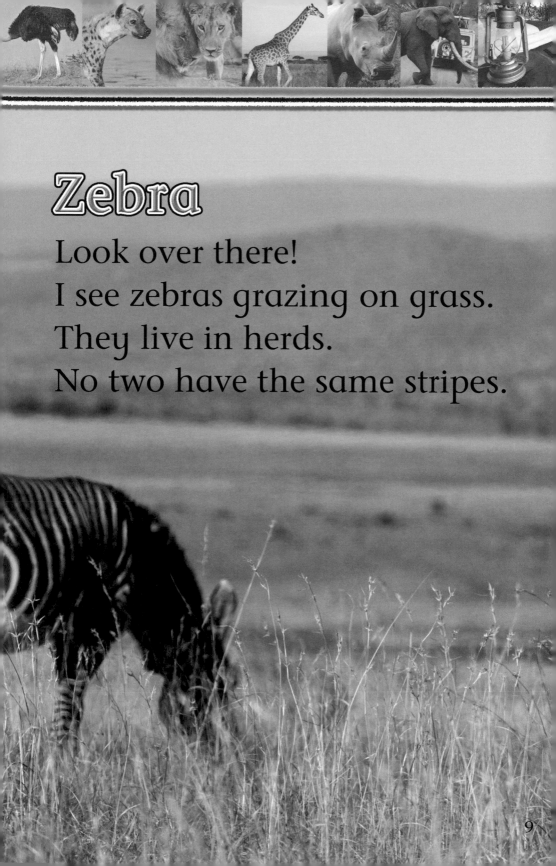

Zebra

Look over there!
I see zebras grazing on grass.
They live in herds.
No two have the same stripes.

Crowned Crane

Look over there!
I see a crowned crane.
Cranes do crazy dances.
They hope to find a mate.

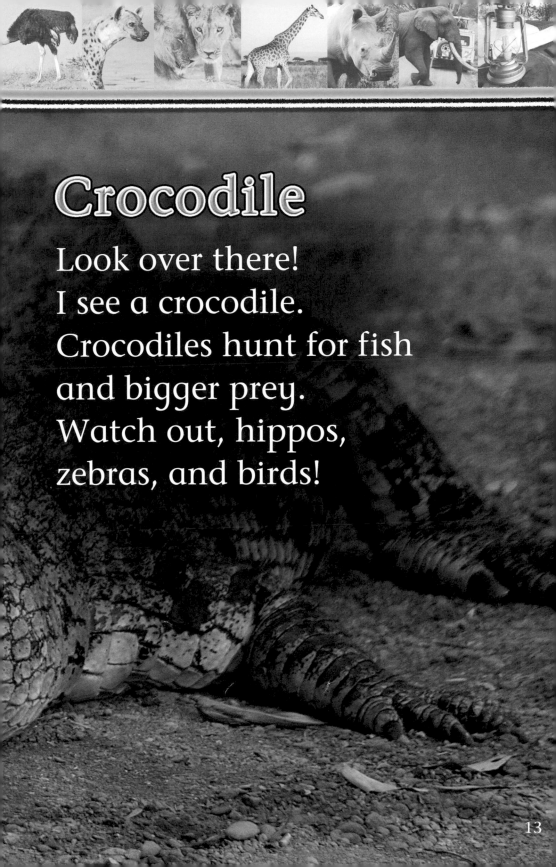

Crocodile

Look over there!
I see a crocodile.
Crocodiles hunt for fish
and bigger prey.
Watch out, hippos,
zebras, and birds!

Buffalo

Look over there!
I see a buffalo.
Males live alone, but
females live in herds.
Herds drive away lions!

Hippo

Look over there!
I see a hippo.
Hippos stay cool in
the water.
Hippopotamus means
"river horse."

Ostrich

Look over there!
I see an ostrich.
Ostriches cannot fly.
Luckily, they are
fast runners.

Spotted Hyena

Look over there!
I see a spotted hyena.
Hyenas live in large groups.
They communicate with a
laughing sound.

Lion

Look over there!
I see lions.
Only males have manes.
Females do much of
the hunting.

Giraffe

Look over there!
I see a giraffe.
Giraffes are the tallest
mammals.
They graze on leaves.

Rhino

Look over there!
I see a rhino.
Rhinos wallow in mud
to keep cool.
Mud keeps bugs away, too.

Elephant

Look over there!
I see an elephant.
Elephants spray water
with their trunks.
Trunks can smell and
grab, too.

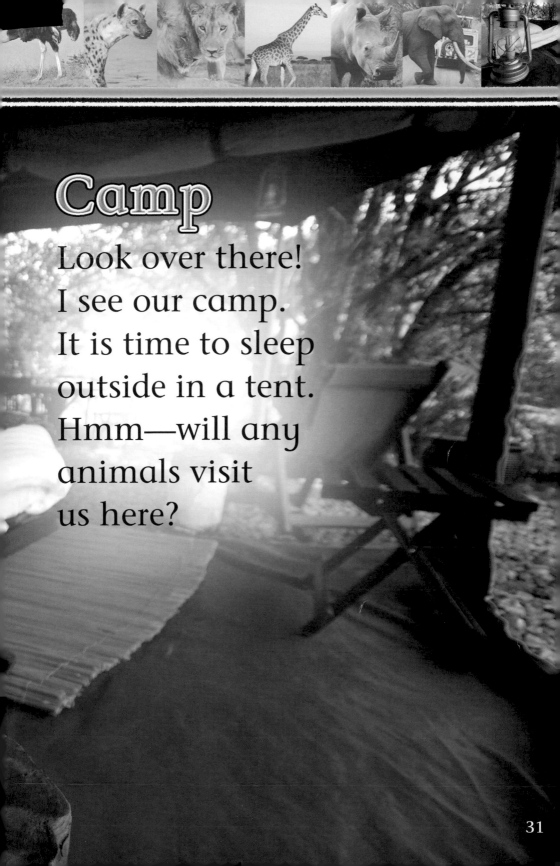

Camp

Look over there!
I see our camp.
It is time to sleep
outside in a tent.
Hmm—will any
animals visit
us here?

GO WILD! African Safari Comprehension Questions

1. Why do leopards have spots?

2. What is interesting about a zebra's stripes?

3. Why do crowned cranes do a dance?

4. Name two things crocodiles eat.

5. What is a group of buffaloes called?

6. Why do hippos stay in the water?

7. How do ostriches get around?

8. What sound do spotted hyenas make?

9. How can you tell a male and female lion apart?

10. What do giraffes eat?

11. Why do rhinos wallow in mud?

12. Name two ways an elephant uses its trunk.